TASMANIA
A ...
TO RE...

Text by Michelle Dale
Photography by Dennis Harding

Dating from 1870 and standing over 48 metres tall, the Shot Tower is a landmark which can be seen for many kilometres down the Derwent estuary. That it remained many more years after its useful life in the production of lead shot was over, is testimony to its value as a monument. The interior circular staircase rises to a balcony at the top and is a challenge for its many visitors.

CONTENTS

Waterfall Valley, Cradle Mountain - Lake St Clair National Park.

TASMANIA

KING ISLAND
Currie • Natacoopa • Grassy

FLINDERS ISLAND
Palana
Whitemark
Strzelecki National Park
Lady Baron
Cape Barren Island

Three Hummock Island
Hunter Island
Robbins Island
Cape Grim
Circular Head
Stanley
Port Latta
Smithton
Marrawah
Rocky Cape Nat. Park
Table Cape
Boat Harbour
Somerset
West Point
Edith Creek
Wynyard
Burnie
Penguin
Ulverstone
Yolla
Turners Beach
Devonport
Port Sorell
Latrobe
Railton
Forth
Asbestos Range Nat. Park
Low Head
George Town
Green Beach
Pipers River
Bridport
Scottsdale
Derby
Mt William Nat. Park
Eddystone Point
Beaconsfield
Dilston
Exeter
Lilydale
Binalong Bay
Sandy Cape
Sheffield
Elizabeth Town
Hadspen
LAUNCESTON
St Helens
Savage River
Waratah
Luina
Deloraine
Mole Creek
Perth
Breadalbane
Evandale
Ben Lomond National Park
St Marys
Scamander
Falmouth
Four Mile Creek
Corrina
Waldhein
Cradle Mtn.
GREAT WESTERN
Longford
Cressy
Fingal
Zeehan
Rosebery
Renison Bell
Cradle Mtn.
Lake St Clair
Mt Ossa
Walls of Jerusalem National Park
Great Lake
Poatina
Conara
Avoca
Douglas Apsley National Park
Bicheno
Queenstown
Lake St Clair
National Park
TIERS
Miena
Arthur Lake
Campbell Town
Lake Leake
Colebrook
Coles Bay
Strahan
Cape Sorell
MACQUARIE HARBOUR
Derwent Bridge
Bronte Park
Lake Echo
Lake Sorell
Lake Crescent
Ross
Tunbridge
Swansea
Freycinet Nat. Park
Franklin - Gordon Wild Rivers National Park
Tarraleah
Bothwell
Jericho
Oatlands
Little Swanport
Schouten Islands
Ouse
Kempton
Melton Mowbray
Colebrook
Triabunna
Orford
Lake Gordon
Mt Field National Park
Bagdad
Spring Beach
Maria Island Nat. Park
Strathgordon
Maydena
Bushy Park
Richmond
Sorell
New Norfolk
Dunalley
Low Rocky Point
Lake Pedder
Huonville
Kingston
HOBART
Eaglehawk Neck
Nubeena
TASMAN PEN.
Port Arthur
South West National Park
Franklin
Geeveston
Cygnet
Barnes Bay
BRUNY ISLAND
Port Davey
Hartz Mtn. National Park
Dover
Hastings Caves
Southport
Adventure Bay
South West Cape
Maatsuyker Group
South East Cape

Approx Kilometres
0 10 20 30

— Road
— Walking Track
National Park
--- Ferry or Cruise
• Power Station

INTRODUCTION

Tasmania's past is a dichotomy of its two peoples, two divergent forces forging dual histories. Yet, Aborigines and Westerners each tell creation stories, both stirring the imagination with strange names and fantastic images.

Fundamental to Aboriginal belief is the Dreamtime, the beginning. Early in the Dreamtime, the island of Trowenna (Tasmania) was enclosed in night until Parnuen, the Sun, rose from the darkness and arced across the sky in a blaze of light. On the second day, Parnuen showered the earth with seeds and rain and, on the third day, he spilled shellfish into the waters. The next day, Parnuen and his wife Vena, the Moon, gave birth to a son, a gleaming white star they called Moihernee.

Moihernee was a great spirit god who reigned over all of Trowenna. He "cut the ground and made the rivers, cleaved the land and made the islands". He then created Parlevar, the man; a figure encumbered with a heavy tail and jointless legs so that he was unable to sit down. Moihernee's brother, Dromerdeem, saw Parlevar's difficulty and intervened to remodel the man's anatomy. He sliced off the tail and healed the wound with daubs of grease then gave the man knee joints and told him to sit on the ground. Parlevar sat and said it was good.

Moihernee, however, was angered by his brother's interference and a tremendous battle ensued between them. Moihernee was hurled to the ground. His wife followed him and together they had many children. Moihernee lived out his days as a man and died in the far South West where he was petrified into a large stone near Cox Bight.

It is history as colourful and dramatic as Christianity which teaches that God created the Earth and everything on it in seven days, and that He sent His son to live as a man upon the Earth. There are even tenuous similarities between the stories. Very little, however, is similar in their philosophies.

Aboriginal spirituality allows for a gentle co-existence with their environment while western civilisation imposes sweeping change. This is not to say that the Aborigines did not modify their surroundings, they did and they did so very effectively. In the Midlands, colonial settlers found grassy, open woodlands unlike the dense undergrowth and forest covering most of the island. This open country was the legacy of the Aboriginal firing regime when fire was their most treasured tool. Even so, in over twenty million years of habitation, little of the country changed in their hands.

The white people, however, came as exploiters. They used the sea and the land, renamed the landscape's features and the land itself. For over 200 years, Trowenna became Van Dieman's Land, named after a Dutch governor; then Tasmania, named after a Dutch explorer because, in 1642, he was the first European to visit these shores.

Later, British explorations paved the way for the first white settlement established in September 1803 at Risdon. Pioneer farmers, whalers and pine cutters came in increasing numbers accompanied by prisoners and soldiers. The state's penal history is dark and grim indeed. The most famous of Tasmanian novels, *For the Term of His Natural Life* by Marcus Clarke, has become a symbol of those cruel times. More tragic still was the violent collision of two cultures, Aboriginal and British, which resulted in near genocide.

From the ashes of this bitter era, there has emerged a stronger spirit, a coalescence of the ancient spirituality of Moihernee and his people, and the modern philosophies of a fair and democratic society. Though their genetic pool may be diluted, Aboriginal descendants still retain their identity. Though the British dominated early white settlement, people of other races are now welcomed to a state which celebrates its multiculturalism. Though they may hold politically opposed views, Tasmanians stand united in their fierce pride and loyalty to this island.

Tasmania straddles the forty-second parallel where it lies exposed to the westerly wind belt known as the Roaring Forties. However, it has not as inhospitable a climate as many Mainlanders believe. Tasmania enjoys the cool Winters and warm Summers of a temperate climate, one of the healthiest and most equable climates in the world. While the wilderness areas of the West and South-West bear the full brunt of the westerlies and the higher peaks are snowladen in Winter, the East Coast is aptly referred to as the "Sun Coast" because it is bathed in warm sunshine for much of the year. Flinders Island is an island paradise which rarely experiences frost while the outlier of Macquarie Island is in the sub-Antarctic region.

Tasmanian life is unhurried and friendly. Visitors often remark on the open, warm hospitality of Tasmanians who are ever willing to stop and help with directions, give advice and/or provide good company. They are considerate and trusting though, in a world increasingly troubled with rising crime rates, these attributes are being tempered with more caution these days. However, even this would not interfere with their desire to help a visitor.

Tasmania is blessed with a wealth of natural beauty and beauty by design, from the splendour of its untamed wilderness to the stalwart and graceful styles of its colonial architecture. Undulating farmlands support sheep with the world's best superfine wool, dairy cattle which produce milk for rich butters and fine cheeses, thoroughbred horses that win major races. Native fauna also have made homes on farmlands, or abound in the dense wilderness areas, or flourish in sanctuaries where they are cared for with affection and widely admired by visitors. English country gardens and stylised Oriental gardens augment the natural flora of the Tasmanian bushland and forest. Peaceful co-existence is emerging as the expectation of this generation, the new creed, the new way of life.

As this century draws to a close and a new millennium dawns, inhabitants and visitors alike are learning to manage wisely and carefully the unique and extraordinary heritage that is Tasmania. It is our future.

Ross Bridge dates from 1834 and is one of the most picturesque of Tasmania's bridges. Convict Daniel Herbert earned a free pardon by sculpturing the 184 unusual celtic carvings which embellish the crests of each arch.

HOBART & SURROUNDS

The South is an area of great diversity and fascinating history. At its focal point is Tasmania's capital, Hobart, the centre from which colonisation radiated outwards, creating a network of settlements throughout the region.

The beginnings of colonisation, however, were hasty and haphazard. The immediate cause of the original settlement was the fear of being forestalled by the French. Alarmed by the appearance of Baudin, Governor King of NSW dispatched Lieutenant John Bowen to found a new colony on the Derwent. This he did in September 1803 accompanied by 49 settlers, 24 of whom were convicts. However, Bowen proved a poor choice. A junior officer less than 20 years old, he lacked the experience to manage convicts and had insufficient authority to discipline unruly soldiers. The site of Risdon was ill-chosen and conditions rapidly deteriorated. With a sense of mounting depression, Bowen risked reprehension by taking it upon himself to leave his post and seek assistance in Sydney. He didn't know that help was already on its way.

In an attempt to remedy the situation, Governor King had dispatched David Collins, with an Order authorising him to supersede. Collins arrived at Risdon in February 1804. He was entirely unimpressed with what he found there and, in less than a week, he had located and removed to an alternate site on the western banks of the Derwent. The move typified his decisiveness and vision. The place he had chosen is the present site of Hobart.

The early years of the settlement were a difficult baptism. The settlers faced severe hardship and many succumbed to starvation because supplies from Sydney were often weeks, even months, late or failed to arrive at all. Governor Collins responded to the problems by proving himself a determined and energetic coloniser. In spite of inadequate equipment, the huddle of tents soon resembled a town with buildings of wattle and daub. In 1808, 554 settlers from the abandoned Norfolk Island landed at Hobart, swelling the struggling population to barely manageable proportions. To alleviate the pressure, Collins dispersed the new arrivals by granting them small parcels of land at Sandy Bay, Sorell, Clarence and New Norfolk. The latter lays claim to the oldest church still in use and the oldest licensed establishment in Australia.

When Collins died in March 1810, times were still difficult but, due to his far-sightedness, the survival and growth of a whole region was ensured.

Succeeding governors oversaw considerable progress. Immigration was encouraged and convict gangs were organised to construct roads, bridges and public buildings. Land was cleared for farming, sheep were introduced and wheat exported to Sydney. Colonial shops plied a brisk trade and docksides bustled with activity.

However, shiploads of convicts continued to arrive and their burgeoning number posed the greatest threat to the expanding colony. From the first, the bonded outnumbered the free. The situation escalated in the four years to 1844 when, of the 15,000 arrivals, less than 30 were free emigrants.

Penal stations were established to accommodate the prisoners, Maria Island was the first in the south and Port Arthur became the most famous. Once ravaged by the corrosive effects of seaside weathering, devastated by bushfires and shunned by the local community, Port Arthur has since undergone extensive and painstaking restoration. With such a calamitous past, it is little wonder that ghosts linger here.

Convicts who served out their sentences were freed to join the settlers and claim land of their own in an ever increasing number of satellite settlements. The small squat cottages and large, sandstone mansions of Richmond, Ross and Brighton provide an insight into their colonial home life.

Visible signs of prosperity abounded. Pubs and taverns appeared closely followed by breweries. Cascade Brewery, at the foot of Mt Wellington, is the oldest in Australia. In response to the needs of the brewers, hops cultivation flourished along the Derwent Estuary.

The social system gradually improved and access to cultural pursuits was bolstered with the establishment of a museum and the Theatre Royal. The latter was a favourite of Sir Lawrence Olivier and Vivian Leigh and still plays host to local and visiting productions.

In the river valleys of the Derwent and the Huon, industry and farming, together with residential development, stamped a new pattern on the landscape. For many years apples were the major crop but now the orchards have given way to fishing, mixed farming and flourishing craft industries. The Derwent also supports secondary industries with the paper mill at Boyer and the Cadbury-Schweppes factory at Claremont.

In the Midlands, vast grazing properties established the island's future prosperity in the production of superfine wool. Some native animals also found the altered landscape to their liking. Brush possums enjoyed the crops and clovers while green rosellas fed on hawthorn hedges.

The maritime influence of the original settlement lives on in the modern pursuits of jet boat riding, white water rafting and water skiing. Yachting is a tradition, never more so than in the Sydney to Hobart Yacht Race which culminates in celebrations at Constitution Dock.

Another race to celebrate its finish at the docksides of Hobart is the international Targa Tasmania. Inaugurated in April 1992, the extraordinary success of this five-day road race will ensure that it, too, becomes a classic event.

From the early days of colonisation to the modern era, Hobart has prospered in the heart of the south. It has overcome the vicissitudes of fluctuating fortunes to become what many hail as the most beautiful of the nation's capitals. Situated in the undulating landscape between the deep waters of the Derwent River and the grandeur of Mt Wellington, Hobart embraces the historic and accommodates the new. It is the focal point of a region which values its past and faces the challenges of the future with a determination reminiscent of its first settlers.

The Hobart Post Office. The growth of the postal system contributed significantly to the development of Tasmania by facilitating reliable communications between the major centres and outlying districts.

Salamanca Place consists of a wharfside row of warehouses built between 1835 and 1860. Transformed into art and craft galleries and restaurants, they form the backdrop to a colourful, open-air market held every Saturday.

The distinctive round tower of Wrest Point Hotel Casino,
the first legal casino in Australia.

Established in 1804, Hobart Town became the centre for the island's government and military. Here the modern city stands in the sights of the past. Kangaroo Bluff Battery was constructed in 1885 as part of the Derwent Defence System.

From 1830 to 1877, Port Arthur was the site of a penal settlement where 12,500 convicts were sentenced for terms ranging from several years to life. Few ever escaped and the Isle of the Dead is a grim testimony that many did not survive their sentences.

Waterfall Bay on the Tasman Peninsula is a popular destination for bushwalkers setting out from Devil's Kitchen. It features spectacular coastal scenery characterised by cliffs composed of vertical, splinter-like columns of dolerite rock.

Fortescue Bay is a remote bay accessible only to bushwalkers and sailors.

At Eaglehawk Neck, the deep colours of sunrise delineate the contours of the extraordinary natural phenomenon of the Tessellated Pavement.

This crossjointing of ancient mudstone was created by erosion along
lines of weakness in the rocks.

The Guard Tower at Port Arthur features in a lantern-lit ghost tour on which the guide relates stories of unexplained occurrences, among them the sound of Reveille - source unknown and undiscovered...

Richmond Bridge, built in 1823, is the oldest bridge still in use in Australia. It spans Coal River and is said to be haunted by more than one ghost from times gone by.

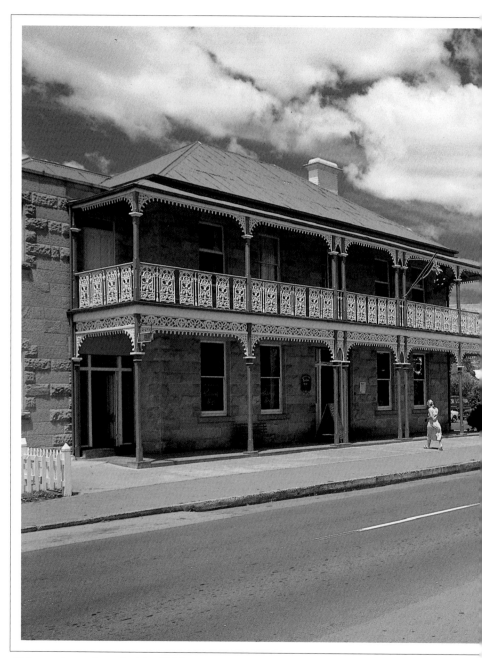

Richmond was founded in 1824 as a convict station and military post of strategic importance. However, since 1872 when the Sorell Causeway was opened, Port

Arthur traffic no longer had to pass through Richmond. The township has seen little development since and has remained much as it was a century ago.

The Bush Mill Railway takes passengers on a 4-kilometre journey back in time. The authentic steam train chugs through native bushland, over the 7-metre high Serpentine Trestle then down to the shores of Stingaree Bay.

This magnificent, purpose-built complex is the Convention and Entertainment Centre at Wrest Point on the Derwent River.

An aerial view of the capital city, Hobart.

At the end of the rainbow is picturesque Bellerive on the eastern shore of the Derwent River.

Historic Cascade Brewery is the landmark and trademark of the Cascade Rivulet which turned the giant waterwheel that powered the brewery. Today the role it plays, though different, is still important to the company - chief bottlewasher !

Victoria Dock, Hobart, is one of the twin docks which are a unique feature in that they bring to the heart of the city all of the colour and activity associated

with small ships. Victoria Dock is also the site of the finish line for the Targa Tasmania, a 5-day car race inaugurated in 1992.

The past shares the skyline with the present: the honey-coloured stones of historic government buildings around Hobart's Parliament Square contrast with the modern high-rises in the background.

The Royal Tasmanian Botanical Gardens comprise a fantastic floral collection which includes English and native seeds first planted in 1829, and 88 rare Asiatic plants presented in 1840. The gardening staff take great pride in caring for the areas allocated to them. The Rose Garden is one such area and features a wide range of predominantly hybrid Tea and Floribunda roses.

Jet boat riding is an exciting way to travel the Huon River and see the Huon-Channel area. Here there is a complete menu of local cuisine ranging from fish and seafood to lamb, vegetables, fruits and wines.

Hastings Thermal Pool is off the Huon Highway near Southport. The pool is refilled daily with warm water from a thermal spring.

Sunrise at peaceful Waterloo Bay on the Huon River.

Russell Falls was originally known as Browning Falls, named after the settler who discovered them in 1856. The three-stage cascade falls in magnificent wide veils over rock estimated to be 220 million years old.

Mount Field is one of the two national parks declared in 1916. They were the first national parks to be officially recognised for their extraordinary beauty.

Battery Point is less a suburb and more of a village, a living heritage recalling old Hobart in its small cottages, elegant houses, shops, galleries and hotels. It is considered to be one of the most complete colonial villages in Australia.

Callington Mill is one of the few remaining relics of steam and wind flour mills, a rare example of a bygone industrial age. Built by John Vincent in 1837, the Oatlands Mill lost its sails when it was gutted by fire more than a century ago.

41

LAUNCESTON & SURROUNDS

The North rivals the South in the fascination of its history and its rich diversity. The seeds of rivalry were sown when Governor King divided the island at the forty-second parallel in order to avoid friction between Collins at the Derwent and Paterson at the Tamar. This formal demarcation of the two regions lasted until 1812 but the rivalry continues to this day. It is a competitiveness which characterises them both in their striving to realise challenging goals, to overcome adversity and to assert their independence. Though they emulate each other in the contest, each has developed a very individual identity and each shows just pride in their achievements. Neither, however, had illustrious beginnings.

Colonisation in the north of the state suffered a more stuttering start than that experienced in the southern region. This task was entrusted to William Paterson who set forth in 1804. The expedition landed at George Town and a small settlement was established there while Paterson continued exploration of the river. Though he considered the present site of Launceston favourable, he eventually chose York Town, near Beaconsfield, as a settlement site because of its proximity to the seaboard. However, as had Bowen's Risdon, the site proved unsuitable and was abandoned in 1806. Paterson moved to the site of his earlier choice, at the confluence of the North Esk and South Esk Rivers. First known as Patersonia, it was renamed Launceston in 1807 to commemorate the birthplace of Governor King.

From its earliest days, Launceston's citizenry displayed enthusiasm and civic pride. They proved to be qualities necessary to the town's survival which now faced contention from George Town. For several years it was uncertain which of the two would become the main establishment. Paterson based his headquarters in Launceston but in 1911, Governor Macquarie instructed its removal to George Town. Less than a year later North and South were united and Hobart declared the premier town. Launceston seemed to be losing out on all fronts. However, the removal of headquarters to George Town was not accomplished until May 1819 and even then it was short-lived. In March 1823, Governor Sorell recommended removal back to Launceston.

Launceston developed quickly. A wharf was commenced in 1820. A number of free settlers took up residence on the fertile land surrounding the town. Stately homes were built, farming land cleared and the villages of Westbury, Hagley, Carrick and Hadspen were settled. Taverns sprang up to take advantage of the large population of itinerant soldiers. A semaphore system connecting Low Head to Windmill Hill in Launceston was set up in 1825. The fastest period of growth in Launceston's history was between 1831 and 1837 when the population increased from 2,500 to 7,185.

Convicts were also accommodated in the region. One working at Morven was a man called Kelly, the father of Ned who became the most notorious of Australia's bushrangers. In honour of Tasmania's first Surveyor-General,

G.W. Evans, Morven became Evansdale in 1836 then later shortened to Evandale.

The bubble of prosperity burst in the 1840s and the whole region struggled through the economic doldrums until tin was discovered at Mt Bischoff. Between 1878 and 1888 it was the richest tin mine in the world and local share holders reaped the profits. Gold was also discovered then coal, copper, silver and lead were added to the region's prosperity.

The boom period encouraged migration to the region. A strong Chinese community settled at Weldborough and a complete joss house survives from that period in the Queen Victoria Museum. Lilydale was formerly known as German Town after the origin of its settlers. Bardenhagen's General Store is still trading there in the ownership of the founder's descendants.

In 1888 Launceston was declared a city and it has continued to be, if unofficially, the capital of the North. Aptly named the "Garden City" for its splendid parks, squares and both public and private gardens, the soubriquet could as well be extended to the whole region. Around Deloraine and beyond, hot house and open air flowers are cultivated to supply local and interstate florists. The Bridestowe Lavender Farm at Nabowla produces scented oils for the great perfumeries of the world and provide an outstanding tourist attraction. A future tourist attraction of great potential is the site of the old semaphore relay station at Mt Direction which offers fabulous views of the Tamar Valley.

Fruit also flourishes in this fertile valley. The apple industry is poised to return to the international export markets with contracts being negotiated with Japan. Delicious nashi fruit are becoming increasingly popular and pears are an old favourite. There are cherry orchards at Gravelly Beach and around Lilydale. There are raspberries and blueberries aplenty and passers-by on the East Tamar Highway are invited to stop and pick plump strawberries at Hillwood. Vineyards are opening a new and exciting chapter in Australian winemaking, producing table wines of international appeal.

Offshore, the islands of the Furneaux Group are home to fishermen, farmers and muttonbirders. Killicrankie diamonds (white topaz) are also found here and the scenery is breathtaking. Sheep grazing extends from Flinders Island to the Midlands. The world's finest wool has been sold for record prices at northern auctions. The oldest woollen mill in Australia was established at Waverley in 1874 and it is still welcoming visitors.

The craft industry thrives in cottage shops and market places. Skills both ancient and innovative are displayed in a myriad of wares. Artists, too, contribute a wealth of talent. Galleries both large and small exhibit collections of paintings, drawings, sculpture and photography worthy of international attention.

Because of the indomitable spirit of its pioneers, Launceston is today the commercial heart of a region rich in history, industry and hospitality. That same spirit is present today in its modern citizens. The past is proudly preserved as a living heritage, a story of success which augurs well for the challenge of the future.

Sunrise from the Midland Highway. Dating from 1819, it is one of our earliest roads.

The National Trust of Australia (Tasmania) was established in 1960 for the specific purpose of acquiring and preserving Franklin House. It was built in 1838 by local brewer and innkeeper, Britton Jones. Extensive Cedarwood woodwork is an outstanding feature of the interior.

The John Hart Conservatory is the focal point of City Park's floral displays. Built by the Launceston Corporation in 1932, it is now in the expert care of the Parks and Recreation Department.

Yorktown Square, in the shopping centre of Launceston, accurately recreates the character and architecture of early Tasmania.

One of the great Georgian houses of Australia, Clarendon was completed in 1838 for James Cox, wealthy woolgrower and merchant. It was the second house acquired by the Tasmanian National Trust when it was given to them by Mrs W R Menzies in 1962.

Established in the early 1800s, Evandale is a picturesque village
featuring many historic buildings. Today it is renowned for the

colour and variety of its Sunday markets and the celebratory
atmosphere of its annual Pennyfarthing event.

The Launceston Federal Hotel combines the luxury of a first class hotel with the full facilities of a casino and country club. Though completed in 1982, its design is reminiscent of grand colonial times.

The Cataract Gorge Restaurant was built in the early 1900s. Its unusual design is worthy of its setting: Victorian gardens embellished with leafy ferns, exotic plants and brilliantly coloured peacocks.

Entally House, built circa 1820, was restored by the Scenery Preservation Board (forerunner to the National Trust) and opened in 1950. An outstanding

success, it became a model throughout Australia for the restoration of country homes. In addition to the house, the property includes farm buildings and a beautiful garden.   55

The Penny Royal Gunpowder Mill is situated in an old quarry site near Kings Bridge. It
56 comprises the only complete set of working gunpowder mills in the world. The

mills, cannon foundry and fort are set amidst gardens, waterfalls and a lake on which sail the 10-gun sloop *Sandpiper*, 6-gun privateer *Pelican* and the cutter *Kittiwake*.

Built in 1840 at Barton near Cressy, the Penny Royal Watermill was relocated stone-by-stone to its present site in Launceston. Completed in December 1972, it became the first building in the Penny Royal Complex.

The *Lady Stelfox* is principally constructed of Tasmanian Oak. Weights were attached to the branches of growing trees to artificially create the line of the ribs. The design of the shallow-draft paddlesteamer was based on Yukon River vessels and is ideal for cruising the Tamar River and Cataract Gorge.

The original span of Kings Bridge was prefabricated in England then shipped to Launceston where it was assembled and floated into place in

1863. An identical span, constructed at a local foundry, was floated alongside in 1904 to provide a second traffic lane.

The spectacular triple Liffey Falls is a major attraction for sightseers and bushwalkers.

Found west of Mole Creek, the Marakoopa Caves are a subterranean landscape of fantastic limestone shapes and textures, and home to Marakoopa glow worms.

Quamby Bluff forms a dramatic backdrop to the township of Deloraine named after Sir William Deloraine in Sir Walter Scott's poem, "The Lay of the Last Minstrel".

Taking special care of our Koala immigrant is a young visitor to the Trowunna Wildlife Park. Koalas are mainlanders and they share this sanctuary with a wide variety of native Tasmanian creatures including free-ranging Bennetts wallabies, pademelons and giant Forester kangaroos; the shy pygmy possum, abundant birdlife, reptiles and Tassie devils.

The Tasmanian devil, a nocturnal marsupial, is unique to Tasmania and is found in healthy numbers throughout the island. While only the size of the average dog, the devil's jaws are among the strongest of any creatures, enabling it to consume whole carcasses of carrion or prey.

The tiger snake is among the most venomous of land snakes. In 1992 the first export license was granted to Mr D Lawrence to breed and rear the snakes for overseas markets, most notably Asia, where their meat, skins and venom are highly prized. The skins are also used to stunning effect by Tasmanian artists Gary Greenwood and Helen Huxley whose work may be seen at the Tasmanian Design Centre, Launceston.

Acres of these beautiful pale poppies (Papaver somniferum) are grown and harvested for their essential medicinal value.

The Bridestowe Lavendar Farm, Nabowla, is among the world's largest producers of flower oil to European and American perfumeries.

Spanning the Tamar River between Sidmouth and Deviot is the Batman Bridge distinguished by a spectacular 100-metre steel A-frame tower. Completed in 1968, it is one of the first cable-stayed truss bridges in the world.

Grindelwald, a village reminiscent of its Swiss namesake, nestles in the gentle hills of the Tamar Valley.

Campbell Town Bridge, built between April 1837 and July 1838, features bricks stamped with the thumb prints of the convict construction crew.

NORTH-WEST & WEST

The North-West and West comprise a region of industrial development and natural beauty. Primary industry is essentially linked to the fortunes of the West while both primary and secondary industries form the economic basis of the North-West. Sandy beaches lure ocean swimmers and sun bathers to the North-Western seaboard while the unparalleled wilderness of the West attracts visitors from around the world. This industrious and leisurely duality of the region characterises a way of life which ascribes equal importance to hard work and relaxation, endeavour and reward.

It is the culmination of an enterprising but often difficult past. The first regional settlement, at Macquarie Harbour, had a brief and bitter history. From 1821 to 1834 it was the island's most notorious penal colony, the entrance to which was aptly named Hell's Gates.

Beyond the dense forest enclosing Macquarie Harbour, little was known of the region prior to 1823 when Lieutenant-Governor Sorell commissioned three expeditions to undertake the search for habitable land. The first was led by Charles Hardwicke who, though impressed with the country around Port Sorell and Circular Head, was dismayed by unsuccessful attempts to penetrate inland. Meantime, John Rolland investigated an overland passage. His attempts, however, were blocked by steep country beyond the Mersey district. Nevertheless, he was the first European to sight Cradle Mountain and Rolland's Repulse, now known as Mt Roland. The third expedition was captained by James Hobbs. At best his report concurred with Hardwicke's findings that the area around Circular Head was by far the most suitable for agriculture. Thus two years of government-sponsored exploration failed to discover much of the hinterland beyond the coast.

It was not until 1826 that the Van Diemen's Land Company became the first to take up the challenge of settlement in the North-West. Financed by British investors, the VDL Co. arrived with surveyor, Henry Hellyer. Within two years Hellyer, Joseph Fossey, Clement Lorymer and assigned convict Jorgen Jorgensen, had triumphed where their predecessors were unable to pass. It was Henry Hellyer's dedicated determination which literally put the rugged North-West quarter on the map.

The first manager of the VDL Co. was Edward Curr who designated Circular Head as the fittest place for their first farming venture and established Stanley as the first settlement. During his fifteen year administration, he withstood crushing adversities with the loss of crops and sheep, and trouble between free settlers and assigned servants. The early survival of the VDL Co. can be attributed almost entirely to the capabilities and integrity of Curr whose rule, though sometimes harsh, was always humane and appropriate to the difficulties of the task.

Those farmers who followed in his spirit battled isolation, dense forest and the elements. Little by little the land yielded to their tireless endeavours. The heritage they left is testimony to their unfailing fortitude, a region rich in undulating farm land. The timber cutters assisted the farmers' cause by clearing tracts of temperate forest. The sawmill on the Don estuary was notable for being manned and supplied by experienced Canadian lumber men. When the business faltered, a new syndicate took over and formed the River Don Trading Company. At its height this remarkable company was able to supply everything from cotton reels to bullock drays and draught horses. It cultivated and processed food, manufactured agricultural equipment and exported to markets as far away as South America. Don was a boom town until the district began to decline and the company moved to Devonport.

James "Philosopher" Smith was the most eminent of the pioneering miners. Well equipped with knowledge and experience gained on the Victorian gold fields, he returned to Tasmania convinced that there were more important mineral deposits in the north-western quarter. He found indications of gold, copper and silver but the great discovery of his life was tin at Mt Bischoff, Waratah. For half a century Mt Bischoff was unchallenged as the greatest tin mine in the world. A curiosity of the field was a small area called Religious Hill. By coincidence, a number of families living there had surnames including Church, Deacon, Parson, Pope and Priest. These days their descendants are more liberally scattered throughout the state.

Ore, however, is a finite resource and many mines are nearing the end of their productive life. The boom towns of yesteryear - Zeehan, Waratah, Gormanston, Linda and others - are but shadows of their former selves. Yet the spirit of the people has not declined. They are survivors. Though new mines have started operation, most notably the Hellyer zinc-lead-silver deposit, the future economy of the West Coast may be more reliant on tourism. Strahan is leading the way with its popular Gordon River cruises and scenic wilderness flights.

Sawmilling remains a major industry though its future, as with mining, must be in careful management of resources at sustainable levels to ensure their ongoing availability. The pulp and paper industry at Burnie is supportive of such planning. Burnie is firmly developed on the Associated Pulp and Paper Mills which is a major employer of the city's population.

Devonport is the home port of the *Spirit of Tasmania*, which handles tens of thousands of passengers a year. Visitors to the state disembark to discover a most attractive city of friendly, helpful locals.

The North-West remains, fundamentally, a region of primary production. Smithton is the centre of a rich dairying district. Potatoes are by far the region's biggest harvest and are mostly grown on contract for processing factories at Smithton, Ulverstone and Devonport. The North-West easily leads the state in the production of dairy products, vegetables and beef cattle.

The region is adorned with fine townships, including Sheffield, Forth, Latrobe, Ulverstone, Penguin and Wynyard. Each has a special charm and impressive history. Theirs is a story of endeavour and reward; the heritage of the North-West and West.

Mount Roland, rising abruptly to 1234 metres, dominates the skyline of the Sheffield district.

For many visitors who arrive by sea, Devonport is the gateway to Tasmania. In recognition of this role, the city established the Devonport Showcase, a complete exhibition centre designed to provide everything from oatmeal muffins to invaluable information about this attractive city and the surrounding region.

The patchwork of red-brown and green of rich farmland near Forth.

Standing in a deep carpet of wild flowers, this bare tree provides a
striking contrast in the scenery near Elizabeth Town.

The Don River Railway Society reconstructed for display the largest collection of steam engines and passenger carriages in Tasmania. They provide a ride along the state's first railway line aboard a genuine vintage train.

The striking War Memorial at Ulverstone. The three linked towers represent the three arms of the combined armed forces.

The white sands and sunshine of Boat Harbour Beach attract both locals and tourists alike to this favourite holiday destination.

Varicoloured displays of springtime wildflowers are a familiar sight by the roadsides of Tasmania. This display decorates the route along the old highway near Penguin.

This mechanically-operated, miniature windmill was built in Hiscutt Park by the Dutch community of Penguin. In Spring, the windmill is surrounded with tulips.

Burnie is an industrial city and the hub of business on the North-West Coast.

This scene of rural tranquillity is found in an urban setting: the view from Bells Parade, Latrobe.

Guide Falls, near Burnie, provides walkers with a scenic resting place and the sweet taste of fresh water.

The Pioneer Museum, Burnie, is a fascinating recreation of an entire early Tasmanian village.

These fascinating water patterns are created by the varying depths of shifting sands in Duck Bay near Smithton.

Sunset over Cape Country, the North West corner of Tasmania.

In the shadow of the Nut lies the historic village of Stanley.

Mount Murchinson forms a majestic backdrop to Bastyan Dam near Rosebery.

The soft sunlight of late dawn suffuses the landscape of
Waratah with gold.

Tasmania is renowned for its production of fine wool, dairy foods, lamb and beef. Here Hereford cattle share grazing land with Polwarth and Corriedale sheep near Sheffield.

The stark, lunar landscape around Queenstown is a legacy of extensive mining and is preserved by the locals as a unique attraction.

Cruising in style on the Gordon River between banks of lush wilderness rainforest.

THE EAST COAST

The East Coast is variously, and appropriately, known as the "Sun Coast" and "Holiday Coast". More than half of its coastal seascape is fringed with white, sandy beaches bordering on sheltered harbours of clear water and separated by rocky outcrops. North from the Freycinet Peninsula, surfing beaches become more sweeping; some extending for many kilometres and owning names such as Seven Mile Beach and Nine Mile Beach in recognition of their length. The climate is warm for much of the year, more equable by far than any other region in the state.

These are the required ingredients for ocean swimming, surfing, sailing and fishing which is why the Eastern seaboard has become so popular as a holiday destination. Holiday houses are commonplace in the picturesque seaside resorts where visitors outnumber locals by as many as five to one in the summer months and school term breaks Though called "shacks" by their owners, many of these second homes are as comfortable and well-appointed as permanent residences found in towns and cities.

Tourism, however, has come latterly to the East Coast. Its settlement by Europeans was in response to very different economic influences though they, too, were drawn here by the desirability of its scenic beauty and congenial climate.

In the early days of colonisation, free settlers chose grants of land around the principal establishments of Hobart on the Derwent River and Launceston on the Tamar. When all the available land around these localities had been claimed, prospective settlers looked to the lightly-wooded hills and native grasses of the eastern half of the state. Generous governors, eager to attract suitable families to what was predominantly a penal colony, instituted the free grants system whereby land was given in proportion to the amount of capital possessed.

Thousands of acres were apportioned to retired officers of the British military or civil services. Many of the properties were like the parklands of noblemen's estates and, with little undergrowth needing to be cleared, abounded in natural grazing pastures ideal for sheep. Assigned convict servants provided what little labour was needed. Except for their rough, pioneering lifestyle and the constant threat form bushrangers, those early settlers might well have believed themselves in The Promised Land.

In the North-East, the landscape is characterised by rolling hills, rugged mountains and high, wide plateaux such as the Saddleback which extends south from Ringarooma to the Fingal Valley. Steep gorges and rift valleys have created challenges for highway engineers and resulted in distinctive features such as St Mary's Pass and Elephant Pass, each winding for six kilometres and eleven kilometres respectively.

Coal seams were discovered in the north-eastern quarter and tin mining ushered into being places such as Derby. This once bustling town has declined since the depletion of its deposits but it still proudly exhibits visible signs of past mining activity, most particularly the Briseis Hole. Named after the 1876 winner of the Melbourne Cup, the Briseis Mine was operated by the Kruska brothers until 1900 when the Briseis Tin Mining Company was formed in London to work the rich deposits further.

Many Chinese arrived last century to work the alluvial tin found in the creekbeds around Coles Bay and the Freycinet area. However, the vagaries of the world market finally brought about the demise of tin mining in Eastern Tasmania just as the cost of production, transport and an uncertain market killed the coal industry. However, it is not forgotten. The past is remembered and celebrated in coal shovelling contests held at the renowned Fingal Valley Festival.

The north-eastern quarter has remained an agricultural district. Potatoes and hops are plentiful around Scottsdale while Ringarooma is the centre of a rich dairy farming area.

On the Eastern seaboard, fishing is the mainstay of the economy. Their maritime history dates back to the days of the whalers, who kept lookouts for waterspouts, the signal for waiting boats sheltering in coves. The whales are few now and the whalers gone. Nowadays it is principally crayfish which interest the fishermen of coastal seaports such as Bicheno, St Helens and Coles Bay. Among the game fish is the giant bluefin tuna and top class table fish include trevally, trumpeter and flathead.

Swansea has developed ideal fishing facilities. Whether from pier, beach, rocks or river, this venue appeals to sporting fishermen nation-wide. A must for visitors to this coastal town is the Swansea Bark Mill, a fully restored working display and pioneer exhibition.

At Triabunna, the Pioneer and Working Horse Museum is step back in time. It offers an insight into Australia's pioneering heritage from farm machinery and horse drawn vehicles to an accurate reconstruction of the local blacksmithing shop. There are animals, too - magnificent Clydesdale horses, tiny Shetland and border collies.

The scenery of the East Coast is magnificent. Steep cliffs of dolerite spires delineate the coastline to spectacular effect. At Coles Bay the outstanding landmark is the Hazards, hills of red granite over three hundred metres high, from which the facings of many Hobart buildings have been quarried. The Hazards are part of the Freycinet National Park, where birds proliferate in the unspoiled bush of this reserve and wildlife sanctuary. Over sixty varieties of ground orchid have been discovered and identified here.

The charm of quiet beaches and inlets is redolent in their names: Sleepy Bay, Friendly Beaches, Wineglass Bay and Honeymoon Bay. Clearly marked walking tracks have increased in number since more and more visitors have set out on foot to discover secluded coves and explore the scenic wonders of this region for themselves. The locals make their visitors very welcome. Their warmth springs from the atmosphere of charm and unspoiled tranquillity that pervades of the entire East Coast.

Maria Island: home to a multitude of wildlife and the site of Tasmania's oldest penal colony.

First built as a house in the 1870s, the Pub in the Paddock was licensed as a hotel in 1906. The pub is famed as a venue for woodchopping competitions which continue on a regular basis in a purpose-built, lighted arena for night chopping. Licensee, Tim Partridge, manages the pub and the menagerie which includes a beer-drinking pig and Elle the wombat.

The steady flow of mountain water through rocky streams and forest pools coalesces into the cascades of St Columba Falls, Pyengana.

The variegated greens of lush rainforest below St Columba Falls, Pyengana.

Deep sea fishing is the primary industry of the East Coast where crayfish and tuna are caught in abundant quantities. Here a cray boat docks at Refit Wharf, St Helens.

Late afternoon sunshine dapples the water of beautiful
Georges Bay, St Helens.

A jetty reaches into Georges Bay, offering a brief walkway connecting land and sea.

This coastline near Scamander is typical of the 'Sun Coast' where many come to enjoy the warm sunshine and white beaches.

The rocky ocean foreshore near Four Mile Beach.

Abounding with top class table fish including flathead, trumpeter and trevally, Great Oyster Bay offers one of the best in-shore fishing spots in Australia.

The panoramic beauty of secluded Wineglass Bay in the Freycinet National Park.

The enchantment of Coles Bay is felt by all its visitors.

On the edge of world-renowned Freycinet National Park, Coles Bay
shelters at the foot of the red granite mountains known as the Hazards.

The Swansea Bark Mill features a very unusual machine made with packing cases, bed sheeting, horseshoes and wool. It was powered by a steam engine and used to grind black wattle bark, an important ingredient in leather tanning. The mill was bought, restored and opened for exhibition in April 1982 by Peter and Jane Lewis.

The history of colonial settlement in the area is recreated in individual displays at the Yesteryear Museum, Swansea.

On board the *Enterprise* at The Sealife Centre, Bicheno.

For visitors to The Sealife Centre, the *Enterprise* offers an educational experience and magnificent views of Waubs Beach, Bicheno.

The dramatic beauty of Coles Bay at sunset.

WILDERNESS

Wilderness is a landscape undisciplined by human hand, unrefined by technology, untouched by any need except its own inexorable evolution. It is and always has been wild, for every day of its multi-million year existence. It is and always has been free, unscarred by roadways, unhindered by traffic, buildings and power lines.

Its present form remains true to its ancient origins and the powers which shaped it: from the violence of earthquakes and eruptions to the gentler forces of wind and rain. Wilderness is spectacular terrain; rich in the volume and variety of life that it supports, unmatched in the sum of its unique components.

Yet it survives against the odds, a wild corner in an industry-driven society subject to relentless economic pressures. Much of the state's wilderness vanished in the wake of those pressures: the profit potential of freely available resources, national and international market demands, the urgency to create more and more jobs. In less than a quarter century since 1950, half the remaining wilderness was lost to industry.

In response, conservationists committed themselves to a collision course with progress. Battle lines were drawn in a conflict which divided the community, involved the federal government and gained international attention when Tasmania's South-West region was nominated for World Heritage listing.

The region achieved a world record by fulfiling seven of the possible ten criteria applicable to heritage sites. Of these seven, its wilderness value is the most significant, a fact commemorated in the official title bestowed upon the area by the World Heritage Committee: "Western Tasmanian Wilderness National Parks".

Only the central part of the wilderness is fully protected and this area comprises the Cradle Mountain - Lake St Clair National Park (131,920 hectares), the South-West National Park (442,240 hectares) and the Franklin-Lower Gordon Wild Rivers National Park (181,075 hectares). The battle to include the surrounding wilderness areas for World Heritage listing continues.

Tasmanian wilderness is characterised by dramatic terrain dominated by fantastic shapes inspiring such names as the Acropolis, The Labyrinth, the Walls of Jerusalem, Frenchmans Cap and The Hippo. The ages of these sandstone and quartzite and dolerite monoliths are counted in thousands of millennia - lengths of time that defy comprehension.

The weather is as daunting as the landscape. With an annual rainfall spanning over 200 days, South-West Tasmania is undoubtedly the wettest region in Australia. Accompanying the persistent rainfall are strong winds, low temperatures and heavy mists. Though the region is famed for picturesque and diverse bushwalking areas, the extreme and rapid changeability of the weather can test the most experienced walker.

In remote, elevated areas, sudden freezing conditions can cause death in an hour.

The vegetation is as prodigious and indomitable as it is curious and unique. The triffid-like pandani (Richea pandanifolia), though ubiquitous in its native Tasmania, is a rare species in global terms. The King Billy pine (Athrotaxis selaginoides) and slow-growing Huon pine (Lagarostrobus [Dacrydium] franklinii), two of the eight endemic conifers, may live beyond 1500 years if their survival is not threatened by fire. Eucalyptus, however, thrive in the aftermath of burning which provides them with the necessary conditions for their regeneration. Without fire, eucalyptus would be gradually superseded by rainforest.

Since World Heritage listing effectively banned logging from protected wilderness sites, different industries have emerged to replace the old. While these new enterprises also take advantage of freely available natural resources, they are more conscious of maintaining and promoting the delicate ecological balance of the region.

The heavy and prolonged rainfall provides a plentiful source of spring water which is bottled on the West Coast. Tasmanian Wilderness Foliage is a company which lightly and selectively culls abundant plants for local and mainland floral, herbal medicine and bush tucker markets. Among the florist foliages are mountain rockets (Bellendena montana), prized for their blazing red beauty; the rainforest myrtle (Nothofagus cunninghamii), noted for its variegated autumnal hues; and the common buttongrass (Gymnnoschoenus sphaerocephalus) gathered from the peat bogs of Cradle Mountain - Lake St Clair National Park. Plants garnered for mainland food markets include the spicy hot native pepper (Drimys lanceolata), the sweet snowberry (Gaultheria hispida) and the cider gum (Eucalyptus gunnii), the fermented sap of which is very like maple syrup. Demand for all that is healthy, wild and natural is ensuring that these new enterprises experience steady growth.

Wilderness areas offer science a wonderful opportunity to study the evolution of our flora and fauna. Fossil evidence supports the possibility that many of our land-based animals evolved in rainforest regions and adapted as the climate changed. In addition to fossil sites, there exist rich archeological sites which provide valuable insight into how early Aborigines survived an inhospitable environment. The interest for, and importance to, the international scientific world highlights the need to protect what remains of our rainforests so that this evolutionary evidence is not lost.

Tasmanians have understood and appreciated the significance of their wilderness areas for more than a century. Tasmania's first scenic reserve, Russell Falls, was declared in 1885, followed by two national parks, Freycinet and Mt Field, in 1916. However, modern history has dramatically illustrated that our responsibility to the land must go beyond holding its treasures in trust and extend to our ability to safeguard them so that their extraordinary and unique qualities remain to be passed onto future generations.

The distinctive outline of Cradle Mountain reflected in Dove Lake.

The Twisted Lakes track is an easy two hour walk around glacial tarns fringed with colourful lichens and alpine heath.

Weathering and erosion have dramatically shaped the columns of the Acropolis in the DuCane Range.

Ancient native forest of Tasmanian deciduous beech (Nothofagus gunnii), the triffid-like pandanis (Richea pandanifolia) and statuesque King Billy pine (Athrotaxis selaginoides).

Pencil pine forests (Athrotaxis cupressoides) abound in elevated areas and provide essential habitats for native fauna.

Quamby Bluff is an 'island' peak standing adrift of the Central Plateau. Rising 1226 metres above sea level, much of northern Tasmania can be seen from the summit.

A plethora of native ferns crowd the banks of Liffey River.

Layers of ancient rock and scorparia on Mount La Perouse provide a dramatic foreground to the stately Hippo in the Southern Ranges.

George Howes Lake is one of four thousand lakes and tarns in the Walls of Jerusalem National Park. The glaciated sculpturing of the region bears a striking resemblance to Norwegian topography.

Included in proposals for World Heritage listing are 11, 510 spectacular hectares comprising the Walls of Jerusalem National Park.

Tasmanian deciduous beech ablaze with Autumn golds among the evergreen foliage of King Billy pines at Fury Gorge.

Wreathed in clouds and shadows, Cradle Mountain dominates a region of wide open moorland and alpine heath.

White-limned pencil pines embedded in the deep snows of Winter on the Central Plateau.

Snow-flanked Cradle Mountain in early morning light.

The mossy undergrowth and green upper storeys of alpine rainforest near Reservoir Lakes in the Southern Ranges.

The aptly named Smoko Creek gushes with snow-melt water which seems
to flow in smokey curls through the wintry forest of the Great Western Tiers.

The thin, twisted branches of bleached wood juxtaposed with the trailing tendrils of pandanis on the north-east ridge of Mount Anne, overlooking Lots Wife.

Like wild, auburn hair, curling tendrils of pandanis shine red in the receding light over Cockscomb Ridge in the Southern Ranges.

Autumn comes to Ballroom Forest, Cradle Mt, in a blaze of colour.

The deep understorey of wilderness forest provide an ideal environment for multifarious mosses and fungi. This colourful cluster was found in Liffey Forest.

Dappled with snow, the dolerite spires of Mount Ossa form an imposing background to the forest of myrtle, King Billy and pencil pines. In the foreground, frosted pineapple grass catches the morning light.

Liffey provides the bushwalker with the prospect of discovering gushing waterfalls amid myrtle trees, wild foxgloves and native ferns.